Sea Otters

by Evelyn Shaw

Pictures by Cherryl Pape

A Nature I CAN READ Book

Harper & Row, Publishers

Library of Congress Cataloging in Publication Data
Shaw, Evelyn S.
    Sea otters.

    (A Nature I can read book)
    SUMMARY: A scientist learns how sea otters live
in the cold Pacific Ocean.
      1. Sea otters—Juvenile literature.
[1. Sea otters.   2. Otters]   I. Pape, Cherryl.
II. Title.   III. Series: Nature I can read book.
QL737.C25S5   599'.74447   79-2017
ISBN 0-06-025613-3
ISBN 0-06-025614-1 lib. bdg.

To Eleanor P. Feldstein,

my mother-in-law

Introduction

Long, long, long,

long, long, long ago

otters lived on dry land.

Then they left the land.

No one knows why.

Perhaps there was not enough food.

Perhaps there was not enough room.

Otters went to live in the water.

Some went to live in the ocean.

There

they found lots of food and room.

They became sea otters.

Sea otters are born

in the cold Pacific Ocean.

They play, swim, and dive there.

They mate there.

They sleep there.

They die there.

Sea otters are mammals
like you and me.
They breathe air.

Scientists want to know about them.

How do they keep warm?

What do they eat?

How do they take care

of their pups?

Chapter I

Susan is a scientist.

She lives in Monterey, California.

She watches a group of sea otters every day.

She sees them do many things.

Today

Susan is sitting in a little boat.

The boat is drifting

toward some plants called kelp.

Kelp is a seaweed

that grows from the bottom

of the ocean to the top.

A sea otter floats
near the kelp seaweed.
Its big paddle-shaped feet
point to the sky.

Susan knows this animal.

She has named her Garbo.

Garbo has a new pup.

Susan has named the pup Bo.

Bo is a few weeks old.

Bo is asleep on his mother's belly.

Garbo is getting ready

to dive underwater.

Bo is not strong enough

to dive.

She leaves her pup

floating in the kelp.

The pup is safe there.

He cannot be seen.

The pup's golden-brown fur

is the same color as kelp.

Bo does not wake up.

Garbo dives underwater.

One minute later

she pops out.

She swims on her back

next to her sleeping pup.

Garbo has found
some food underwater.
She holds five snails
on her chest.
She also has a rock
under her arm.
Garbo cannot bite
into the snail shells.
They are too hard.
She puts the rock
on her belly.
She bangs the snails
against the rock.

She is using the rock

as a tool.

When she gets the snail shells open,

she sucks out the meat.

As she eats

she rolls over and over

in the water.

Pieces of shell fall off.

Garbo also cleans bits of shell

from her fur.

Then Garbo wipes her face
and her whiskers.

She rubs and combs her fur
with the claws on her paws.

She blows into the fur.

Her fur fluffs up.

It becomes soft and airy.

Fluffy fur helps Garbo float.

Fluffy fur keeps Garbo

dry and warm.

Under her fur

Garbo's skin never gets wet.

That is why

Garbo and other sea otters

do not get cold

in the cold ocean.

Now Garbo puts the drowsy Bo,

facedown,

onto her belly.

She is going to feed the pup.

She feeds Bo many times each day.

Bo's mouth touches a nipple.

Bo sucks milk.

Soon Bo falls asleep again.

Little pups sleep a lot,

like little babies.

Then Garbo cleans Bo.

She licks the pup all over.

She fluffs Bo's fur, too.

As she cleans Bo,

she coos, *ku, ku, ku, ku.*

A little while later

Garbo goes to sleep in the kelp.

She lays a kelp ribbon

across her belly.

The kelp ribbon holds her

in one place.

In that way
she does not float far away
while she naps.
Nearby a male sea otter,
other females,
and their pups nap, too.

Garbo wakes up

late in the afternoon.

She hunts for food again.

28

Susan has found

that sea otters eat

abalones, crabs,

sea urchins, and snails.

Sea otters look for food

during the day and at night, too.

Sea otters sleep during the day
and at night, too.
Kelp ribbons cover them
as they float asleep in the ocean.

Chapter II

One morning

Susan plans to dive underwater

to watch Garbo there.

Susan never dives alone.

Her friend, Simon, joins her.

Susan and Simon put on

rubber suits.

Rubber suits keep them warm.

They put big flippers
on their feet.

Flippers make it easier to swim.

They put big tanks of air

on their backs.

Then they can breathe underwater.

Lastly,

they put on glass face masks.

Then they can see very well.

Together,

they swim down.

They swim past kelp ribbons.

The ribbons move to and fro.

It is very beautiful

and very quiet.

Susan and Simon rest on a rock underwater.

They wait for Garbo.

Susan wants to watch Garbo find food underwater.

Soon Garbo swims down.

She swims like a whale,

moving her body up and down.

Garbo chases a crab.

The crab slides sideways.

She does not catch it.

Then Garbo sees an abalone

stuck to a very large rock.

She picks up a smaller rock.

She hits the abalone.

It loosens.

She puts it against her chest,

and she holds it.

She goes up.

Ten minutes later Garbo returns.

This time

she picks up a sea urchin.

The sharp spines do not seem

to bother her.

Suddenly

Garbo sees Susan and Simon.

She swims slowly toward them.

She stares.

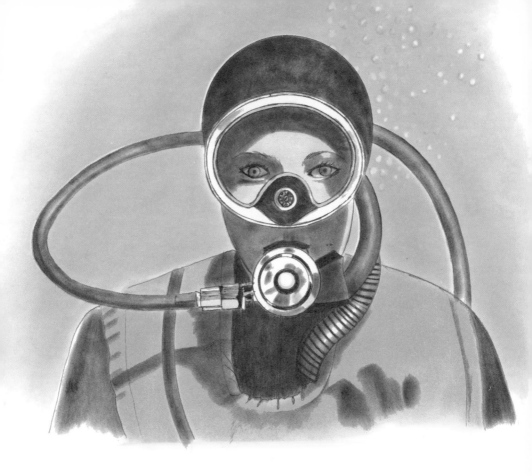

Susan is pleased to meet Garbo
face to face.
But Garbo turns quickly
and swims away.
Garbo may have been afraid.

Susan and Simon swim up

and climb into their boat.

They are happy to take off

their rubber suits and air tanks.

Susan takes Simon to shore.

Then she goes back.

Chapter III

Later that day

the wind begins to blow.

The wind makes the water

rough and foamy.

The boat bounces

up and down in the waves.

Susan is watching Garbo.

Garbo is going to hunt for food.

She puts Bo near the kelp.

The big waves carry Bo away

toward a rock.

Garbo is underwater

for only one minute.

But when she comes up,

she cannot find Bo.

Garbo is very upset.

As she swims,

she looks from side to side.

She is looking for Bo.

Garbo hears little cries.

Waah, waah, waah.

The cries sound like

a pup's cries.

Garbo starts to swim toward them.

But the cries come from a sea gull.

Sometimes sea gulls sound like pups.

Garbo swims near some seals.

She passes big black birds

sitting on a rock.

Just then

Garbo hears little cries again.

Waah, waah, waah.

Garbo screams.

She swims behind the rock.

There is Bo.

Bo does not stop crying
even though his mother is near.

Pups are like that sometimes.

Bo is safe now.

Bo is too little

to live in the ocean

without a mother.

Chapter IV

Bo stays with his mother
for about eight months.
During that time
Susan watches Bo learn
how to live in the ocean.

Bo learns to dive

when he tries to follow Garbo.

At first

the pup kicks up his feet.

Only his head goes down.

Bo tries and tries

and sometimes cries.

The pup cannot dive down.

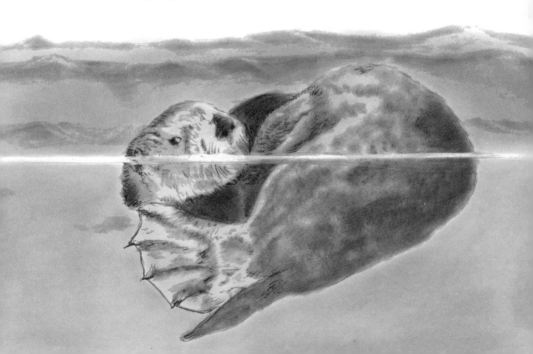

Bo finally learns to dive
when he is a little older,
a little bigger,
and a little stronger.

Meanwhile, Bo learns to swim.

Garbo puts Bo belly down.

Then she swims slowly away.

Bo tries to follow her.

Soon

Bo paddles with his feet

and forepaws.

In a few weeks

Bo swims on his back

and on his belly.

Bo grows bigger.

He still tries to suck milk.

Garbo feeds Bo

pieces of abalone, crab,

snail, and sea urchin.

Sometimes

Bo tries to grab food from Garbo.

Then Garbo may turn away from him.

Bo must learn to find his own food.

Now Bo dives with his mother.

At first

Bo brings up empty shells,

bits of seaweed, rocks,

and plastic cups.

Nothing good to eat!

Later Bo learns

what food looks like underwater.

Then Bo brings up snails

and other food.

Bo tries to open the snails.

He takes his mother's rock.

He taps and taps

but not hard enough.

The snails do not break.

Soon Bo learns to hit

the snails harder.

Bo cleans himself.

He fluffs up his fur, too.

Sometimes

Bo plays with other pups.

They tumble and roll in the ocean.

If they get rough,

their mothers pull them apart.

At night

Bo sleeps near his mother.

He is almost as big as she is.

At the end of eight months

Bo leaves his mother.

He knows how to live in the ocean.

He joins a group of male sea otters.

They float together.

Susan watches other mothers

and other pups.

She sees other mothers do

the same kinds of things

that Garbo did.

61

Susan has learned

how sea otters take care of their pups

in the cold Pacific Ocean.

The scientific name of this species is *Enhydra lutris.* So few otters live near the shores of California now that someday soon they may all become extinct.

The author and artist thank Judson E. Vandevere and Friends of the Sea Otter for use of their excellent resources.